Create Your Purpose, Manage Your Time

a simple guide to increasing productivity and achieving your goals

Kelly Fryer

First printing: 2014

ISBN-13: 978-1503016354
ISBN-10: 1503016358

British Cataloguing Publication Data:
A catalogue record of this book is available from
The British Library.

Also available for Kindle from Amazon.

Other Books by the Author

The Authentic You: Not Just for Leadership but for Life

2014 – My Chrysalis – Release date February 2015

This book is dedicated to my Angels

Acknowledgements

Having never written a book before, I am sure that there should be an order in which the book is written, i.e. the book should be written first, followed by the acknowledgements, so I am probably going completely against the grain, but that's me – although there is a reason to my madness.

I, as I'm sure some of us do, need a reason, a reminder if you will, as to why I sometimes do things. Without this, I can put things off until tomorrow, or until some later point in life, and whilst I have written this book based on not putting things off, as you read it you will see that purpose features quite heavily. I have no doubt, however, that my first draft of acknowledgements will have been extended by the time you are reading them as more amazing people come into my life.

I want to start by thanking Dr Sam Collins, CEO and Founder of Aspire for somehow coming into my life at the right time and inviting me to my first Aspire event, after which I knew that starting my own business was the way forwards. I had no idea though at the time that it would happen so quickly. Sam and Aspire have been a key part of my journey ever since, through Group and One to One Coaching, other Aspire events and by inviting me to be a speaker and mentor at their events. Through Aspire I have met and built long term friendships with some absolutely fabulous people.

Secondly I would like to thank Jackie Perkins for taking the time to find out about me, believing in me, promoting me to her network and inviting me to attend a BeCollaboration meeting where I was able to meet Baiju Solanki. This book had been a thought, a seed and literally not a lot more than a title with some thoughts and content that I couldn't get out of my head. The words had not made it to the page, but Baiju gave me a deadline to complete this, based on an event we were jointly organising, and without that deadline this would not be in your hand.

I want to thank the 'Diversity Tribe' – they know who they are – for their kind words, encouragement and support and for allowing me to find my inner emotions. Emotions have formed an important part of my life, but had for a long time been bottled up and ignored. They allowed me to show them and use them positively and this has helped me hugely in all aspects of my life.

To Gail Thomas, to whom I was introduced by the talented and inspirational Charron Pugsley-Hill, who has guided, challenged and pushed me to succeed. I'm lucky to know you both.

To Alison Thompson, the Proof Fairy, for her diligence and editing skills, without which you would not have this book in your hands.

To all of my friends and colleagues, past and present, that have shaped some of my decisions and allowed me to be me. Admittedly I have always been like Marmite: love me or hate me. To those that do love me and have stuck around, thank you.

To Bowser, my Bulldog, who has followed me round the house and provided a much-needed listening ear at times of despair. He has never left my side and always listens attentively to my crazy ideas.

To Darran, Ben and Jody: although we are very different and don't see that much of each other, I love you all. It's good to be different! Despite a difficult year Jody is still my colourful ray of sunshine.

To Mum and Dad, who have always supported me, despite the

many challenges I have provided them with over the years. All they have ever wanted was for me to be happy, and I am – very. I love you.

To my husband Rob. We have loved each other, but had a lot of times over the years where we didn't like each other very much. Without you I could not have moved my career forwards as quickly as I did, started Chrysalis or had time to write this book. I know that I can be an absolute nightmare – thank you for hanging in there and allowing me time and space when I needed it and a hug and a beer when I didn't.

And lastly, thank you to my two beautiful sons Callum and Robert, the best surprise I could ever have had. You have driven me to succeed to ensure that you have the best start in life to set you up for your future. I am so proud of the young men you are growing into and look forward to seeing the grown men you will become.

Contents

Introduction   15

Why my time is precious   23

Find your why   37

Know your strategy   47

The right mindset   59

What's in your toolbox?   71

Who are your angels and your vampires?   79

Who is holding you accountable?   89

What can you say no to?   95

Summary   103

About the author   105

You know all those things you've always wanted to do?

You should DO them.

Introduction

I remember when I was a child, hearing people talking about life beginning at a certain age. Life begins at forty, then fifty became the new forty, sixty became the new fifty, etc., etc. Films such as 'The Bucket List' show a humorous side to doing all the things you want to do before you leave the earth, but why do we wait? Because there's always tomorrow – or so we think.

As a child, my favourite book was Alice in Wonderland, and the Walt Disney film brought it even more to life. Alice in her pretty dress with her Alice band in her hair. Her daydreaming, and the way she was clearly so different from her family. The Mad Hatter, the Cheshire Cat, the Queen of Hearts, the Caterpillar – all made in their own unique way. And the Rabbit, the one that first catches Alice's attention as he runs after time, not wanting to be late, Alice chasing after him, her curious mind wondering what it is that he was running late for. The entire story is based on time: people being too slow, too fast, the oysters that run out of time too quickly, the Caterpillar, the Hatter and the Hare, all with all the time in the world.

In his uplifting TED talk on gratitude, Louie Schwartzberg speaks of treating each day like it is your first and also your last. What would you notice, what would you do, feel and experience if this were the case? If today truly was your first and last day on this planet, how would you live it?

For Mother's Day, Robert bought me a DVD, 'About Time'. If

you haven't seen it yet you should, and I won't ruin it for those that haven't, other than to say the dad lives each day twice, once with the drama and the normality, the second time noticing all of the small things in life – the chances, the smiles, the things he is grateful for. The son lives each day once, making the most of every opportunity that is presented to him, acknowledging and appreciating everything that is going on around him and never missing an opportunity.

When you hear or watch something inspirational, you often feel like you want to make a change, but more often than not, we put off that change until tomorrow and it is rare that tomorrow comes for us to make the change. Why?

Because when tomorrow comes, we don't stop and allow ourselves the time to implement the change. We get straight back into our lives because there is 'stuff' to do. Like hamsters, we get straight back onto the wheel and keep running to keep things turning. We try to keep up with the pace of life, we try to respond to the emails, the phone calls, the meeting requests, waiting and hoping for everything to slow down so that we can take a breath, make a change and get a greater balance. We can always finish the report tomorrow, leave work early to have dinner with our families tomorrow, go to the gym tomorrow.

The reality, however, is that only we can slow the pace and take the time to get off the wheel, reflect, and make a change today. It's up to us to stop time running away before time runs away from us.

So let's say that you are going to treat today as your first and last day on earth. Do you think 'What's the point, what can I genuinely achieve in a day?' or do you make the most of every precious second, every minute and every hour, knowing that whatever

CREATE YOUR PURPOSE, MANAGE YOUR TIME

legacy you leave behind will have made an impact on you and those around you? Maybe in that one day you'll achieve something so great that it makes a positive impact that sends ripples across the world and makes a real difference. Maybe you will only be remembered by a few people, but still – what difference could you make in a day?

If this is already sounding completely bonkers I make no apology. I'm also not claiming to be the perfect person that has never or will never again put something off until tomorrow. We are all human, right?

Life gets in the way of the to-do lists on occasions; sometimes things crop up out of nowhere, time flies too quickly, there are just not enough hours in the day BUT how much of your life do you wish away? How much time do you waste? How much are you putting off until tomorrow that you could be doing today?

As a child I remember the summer holidays seeming like they lasted a lifetime. The first few weeks were great – you got to go out with your friends, have time away with your family, visit relatives and so on. Then the time came for you to buy your school uniform and all of your new stationery, and you couldn't wait to get back to school because you were bored. And then you stayed bored thinking about going back to school. Then, after a few weeks back at school – and this happened whether you enjoyed school or not – you couldn't wait until the next holiday, and if you were anything like me you would be counting down the weeks you had left until you had more time off. Christmas would be just around the corner, or a party, or a birthday, or a day off, or some other event in your life, and you would start counting down again, wishing the next few days, weeks or months would just hurry up so the day you were looking forward to would be here.

And it's nice to have something to look forward to, right? At the age of 13 I couldn't wait to learn to drive, move out and see the world, get a job. And I had ambition, drive and determination (I still do) but as you get older, things get put on hold, or the 'tomorrow' effect kicks in.

How many times have you told yourself on a beautiful sunny day, 'I will do the gardening tomorrow' and then it rains when tomorrow comes and you wish you had done it yesterday?

How many times have you promised to start going to the gym 'tomorrow', or start dieting 'tomorrow' or start writing your book 'tomorrow'?

How many times have you put off making a difference in your life until after the New Year, or after Christmas, or when you get back from holiday, or after you are married, or when the kids start school, leave home, get married, months if not years in advance?

How many times have you put off a conversation, a meeting, a performance review, setting those budgets until 'tomorrow', because something cropped up, or it wasn't the right time and then you either didn't do it at all, or it was a last minute rush resulting in a poor attempt that won't provide what it needs to do?

This book is not a miracle maker: it won't stop things interfering with your plans, it won't stop there ever being a time when tomorrow has to be the soonest that you start things, but it will give you some guidance on how best to progress. That said, this is not a book on how to manage your to-do list in a more productive way or plan your day more efficiently. It's about finding your purpose, looking at the bigger picture, making the most of what and who you have around you and saying no, so that you are in control of your time and managing it effectively.

Don't let tomorrow be the earliest that you start living, don't let tomorrow be the day you start to make a difference, don't let tomorrow be the day you start doing what you could have or should have done today, because one day, there will be no tomorrow. One day there will only be today.

Primarily, this book is based on principles that may work best in the workplace. Too much structure and planning outside of work can at times stop us living in the moment, stop us from being spontaneous and stop us from being grateful for everything we have around us.

Having a goal, a purpose, a dream or an aspiration is great and this book is for those of you that want to make a difference, to move forwards and to take action in your lives – but reading it and saying you will start tomorrow is not the aim. Without action, this book just looks good on the bookshelf or your ereader.

My wish for you, whether you love or hate this book, is that today – not tomorrow, today – you take a step, maybe a leap, maybe just a movement – something, anything – that moves you forward in some way, shape or form towards your vision, your goal or your dream. That today you do something that takes you along your path towards your destination.

It doesn't matter how big or small you aim, but aim big, aim high and get moving. 'Aim for the sky and you'll reach the ceiling. Aim for the ceiling and you will stay on the floor' – Bill Shankly.

I hope you find reading this book as helpful as I did writing it and that some small nugget of information will stay with you.

When you are finished with the book please pay it forwards – pass it on to someone else who can use a helping hand in taking action today. Let's get as many people living today as we can. Let's get people moving.

Time is precious, don't waste it.

What will make you do something today that will make you proud in a year?

Why my time is precious

At the time of starting this chapter, I am sitting at home having spent the afternoon with a business coach called Becky. Becky specialises in 'reading the minds of customers', allowing business owners/directors etc. to identify what they can do to appeal to more customers.

Our conversation started with her asking me a series of questions about three brands that really resonate with me and then we got onto the topic of my favourite childhood book or film, and we discussed Alice.

The connection between my three brands and the story of Alice was the concept of time. My three favourite brands are all British, all provide quality, all recognise and celebrate their heritage, but for me they offer one thing that I rarely get anywhere else – time. My three favourite brands have all taken the time to find out what their customers want, and this allows me to not waste time when I go there. I know they will have what I want when I want it; I know the items I purchase from them will last, saving me time in replacing them; I also know that if I have the time to browse, ask questions, and find out more to inform my buying choices, they will give me their time to assist my decision.

As a child, I grew up too quickly. The oldest of three to my parents, I was always 'big sister', and for me this meant looking after – or later on, bossing around – my brother and sister. I wanted to be older, I wanted more responsibility, I wanted to grow up – and I did. By the age of 10, I was no longer a 'child' but a young adult and already facing the reality that I was growing much faster than many of my friends. I was viewed differently because of changes to my physique and, far too quickly, I lost the childishness that I should have been holding onto.

Regrettably, I started smoking and drinking in my early teens, as well as going into bars, clubs and pubs – to this date, I have never been asked for ID in the purchase of anything – and I grew up too quickly. This caused a later rebellion against myself rather than anyone else in my late teens, and then before I knew it I was in a job and then I became a parent.

I don't really remember much about my maternal grandparents, I never met my paternal grandmother and by my mid teens, having already lost a childhood friend to leukaemia, I had no grandparents left at all. By the time I was twenty, three 'kids' I had known and been friendly with had all passed away, but it wasn't until I was in my early twenties that I really began to see things differently.

Until then, I had always put things off, or thought about doing something in so many years' time, or wished away where I lived, the working week, counted down to holidays.

At the time I worked as a retail manager and the years really did fly by. In retail you are constantly looking at next month, next season, the next sale, planning for Christmas in July and filling the shop floor with Christmas stock in September. In October you are already looking at rotas for January and in January you are planning for Easter, having spent the last 12 weeks counting how many shopping days are left during the year.

By the age of 24 I was already a parent. I loved my job and the company I worked for, but having been told it would be at least six years before I was able to be promoted due to changes to the structure, I suddenly saw that in six years' time I would be 30 and my sons would be 10. I questioned whether I could wait and take the sideways moves that I had been offered but as much as I wanted to stay, I just felt the next six years would be a waste and I questioned how I would feel in six years' time. I could see that I would gain more experience, but I couldn't see me being happy, climbing the career or the housing ladder or being the best mum I could be for my sons if I didn't take a leap and leave. At this current time I am six years away from forty and I have big plans between now and then, taking a step each day to get me there.

The next two years were madness and mayhem as I tried to figure out whether I wanted to specialise in HR or L&D. I fell into a couple of roles that, although they provided the stepping stones for the rest of my career, were not all I hoped they would be.

At the age of 26 I began a role that allowed me to gain six promotions in six years at two different companies. I led teams, I supported senior leadership teams, I supported and led change, I gained qualifications and experience. I loved my job – and I mean I really couldn't wait for Monday to get back to work – but there was always something that bothered me, and that something is still endemic in many of us today: the lack of time. Be it as individuals, in companies, as leaders or at home, time – the amount we waste, the little value we place on it and the more we wish we had – plays a pivotal role for all of us, whether we like to admit it or not.

Being in a senior HR role, I was privy to a lot of confidential conversations that go on in businesses and I'm not about to break any of those confidences, but I constantly heard and still do hear employees and managers talking about how they didn't have time. They didn't have time to go back to customers, didn't have time to respond to emails, didn't have time to carry out the one to one meeting or performance review, didn't have time to pick someone up on their poor attitude or continued lateness, no time for lunch, too little time at home – the list is endless.

At the time, being a smoker and in an HR position, I also heard many debates about banning smoking breaks as 'smokers' waste far too much time smoking outside and not enough time working.

My experience in this battle, however, was always won by what I noticed and what I experienced myself. As a then smoker, I would take shorter or no lunch breaks, start a little earlier or finish a little later. A five minute comfort break in a meeting gave me just enough time to pop outside, followed by a quick visit to the facilities, and I still managed to get back into the meeting room before many others. Many of the non-smokers would spend 20 minutes making themselves and their team cups of tea, have chats about non-work related things, spend forever in the facilities, take 20 minutes to turn on the computer, make themselves another cup of tea, maybe have a bit of breakfast at their desk and finally, an hour after they arrived for work, they actually started working.

There are then the times that I have sat in meetings that are due to start on the hour and 20 minutes later you are still waiting for the last person to arrive and then you run out of time to cover the agenda and have to arrange another meeting about the meeting you didn't have. Badly chaired meetings that did actually start on time rarely finished on time and I found myself having to make my apologies to get to my next meeting on time, or ended up being late for my next meeting if I could not be excused.

One of my Chief Executives, for all his funny habits and quirks, would always start a meeting on time and you knew that if you were not there for the start time, you may not be allowed in the room. He would say that a train would not wait for passengers and so if you were not on time you had missed the train. If he knew, however, that you had good reason to be late and gave apologies in advance you would be allowed to participate.

When a meeting starts late, those attendees that value their time and are catching up on emails via laptops or mobile devices, or back at their desks, or continuing with work, can sometimes be admired, but then they are rarely present during the meeting because of the delay, so the pattern of valuing everyone else's time more than mine continues. When I say not present, I mean that they are then engrossed in the piece of work or email that has caught their attention and, given that other meeting attendees were not physically there at the start of the meeting, they continue with whatever has their focus at that time. Or even worse, now that technology seems to be common in many meeting rooms, they are constantly on their phone or checking their emails throughout the meeting. Time spent focusing on the actual meeting is rare – what a waste of time!

There was a senior director I worked with once who would use the phrase 'So you think your time is more important than mine?' to anyone who showed up late to a meeting with him. Unfortunately, the fact that he was always late for meetings, late for work, left early every night and never worked on a Friday set the tone for people arriving late for his meetings as they never genuinely believed he would be there in the first place. Not a great reputation.

Another senior director who was responsible for a culture change project I was leading was comical. She was never on time and always allowed meetings she chaired to run over, yet her self-awareness was such that she would say, 'I know I am setting the example and it was unfortunate that I was late today.' The fact was she was late every day and the culture change she was responsible for became a bit of a mockery with her 'do as I say, not as I do' attitude. Not a great ambassador for respecting the time of others.

Then there are the consultants, in the same or similar fields to me, who always tell you they will save you money when you have invested lots of your time and money with them. You will have come across the sort at one time or another. They ask you to arrange or attend focus groups to identify what it is that you need to change, and then they pull something out of a drawer that fits their model but isn't really fit for YOUR purpose. You realise you are paying them a lot of money so they must have your best interests at heart and so you go along with it, only to be redesigning or re-implementing something else six months after they have left. This is something I am proud to say we do not do at Chrysalis. We genuinely value our clients' time and money and only design the right solution for them. Whilst experienced and knowledgeable, a 'one size fits all' approach does not fit all. We provide a tailor-made solution for every single client. Sales pitch over!

Taking it away from work, my mum, who I love dearly, is always late; we joke that she will be late for her own funeral. She knows she will be late; she tries to tell herself and those of us that are waiting for her that she will be on time but she is always late. My dad and I have tried to tell her what the time is when the big hand points to one number on the clock and the little hand to another, but I have gotten in the habit of giving her a time 15 minutes earlier than we need to be somewhere or arriving at hers especially early so I can ensure she is on time. In her defence she is getting much better and does usually make it on time now – usually. She has, however, never missed a train, a plane, a cruise or an important appointment.

Your time is precious and important and so is mine, and whether you run your own business, work for yourself, are employed, a leader, a CEO or a stay at home parent, we have all had times when we wished for more hours in the day, more days in the week and more months in the year.

Stuff, life, time – it happens. You can't stop it, but you can be more effective with what you have. You can value this precious thing, the thing that you will never get back unless of course time travel becomes a reality. You can respect the time of yourself and others and manage your time effectively.

I have built my company on the values that are dear to me, but possibly even more importantly, I built it knowing that my team and I would be ethical. We wouldn't waste our or our clients' time, money or energy on something that doesn't suit them. If we can't help clients we tell them and if necessary we find them someone that can.

The coaching, development, HR and culture change we provide is based on giving our clients the tools and mindset to allow them to be more efficient and more effective. By enabling them to use it more effectively, we give clients the gift of time.

You can always earn more money if you have wasted it or overpaid for something, you can always get more sleep or change your diet to get more energy, but you can never get back time: when it's gone, it's gone.

Can you think of a time when you were at the cinema, a concert, maybe the theatre, and after a few minutes you knew, you just knew that this was going to be rubbish? You told yourself you would wait a bit longer as it might get better and you continued to sit there, clock watching, waiting for things to improve. You sat there thinking, 'I have paid £X for this, I'm not wasting my money!' and you still sat there, waiting, clock watching because it wasn't getting any better. The feeling you had at the start was right, but you had paid and you wanted your money's worth. Then as soon as you stepped foot outside, you heard yourself saying: 'I cannot believe I have just wasted the last two hours of my life, and I will never get them back.'

Often we allow the monetary side of things to inform our decisions a little too heavily. Depending on where you went and when you went, those cinema tickets may have been less than £10, or perhaps you paid upwards of £100 for a concert or the theatre. Over those two or three hours then, what was your hourly rate? £5, £50, more? How long might it take you to earn that money again? You will know the answer to that – I won't even begin to hazard a guess as I don't know how much you earn, but you will know how long you need to work to get back your money.

How will you get back the time?

Quite simply, you won't. It's gone. And you can't just go out and earn some more. It's gone, forever. Unless, like in the 2011 film 'In Time', we find a way to earn more, it has gone.

It saddens me to think that so many of us place a higher value on money than on time. No doubt we have all lost someone close to us at some time in our lives; we can't ever get them back. Do you ever wish you could have just one more conversation with those you have lost, just one more day to tell them everything that you could or should have done when they were here? What would you say, how would you feel?

Time and time again I have heard people say they would give up everything they had just for one more day with a lost loved one. Often we only realise what we had when it's gone.

How many of us have lost money, wasted money, maybe had some stolen? I fit in all three of those categories, and even though at the time it's difficult to deal with, you realise it's only money. You still have your family, friends, health and happiness and that's all that really matters, yet we still waste time every day.

We waste it waiting, procrastinating, worrying, dealing with stuff – non-important stuff, stuff that someone else could have dealt with. We waste it doing things we don't like in jobs we don't enjoy. We waste it wishing our lives away, not taking action until after some big event, and then still continue to waste time not doing what we wanted because we are waiting for something else. Before we know it, we have wasted years waiting for the promotion, or to start our own business, and the kids have grown up and left home and we look in the mirror and we don't recognise the person staring back at us.

Think about the team members you didn't support because you didn't have time that have now resigned, or worse still have stayed and are ineffective. The customers you didn't have time to serve that have left dirty footprints over every digital and social media format possible containing details of the poor service levels they received. The relationships you wasted, the kids you never had, the training you never did, the qualification you never started, the book you never wrote ... it's all there in your mind, going around and around as you ask yourself 'What if?'

For each of us, time is precious. For each of us it will mean different things. Some of us are waiting for something with a very good reason and/or a very good intention, but many of us are not. We are just wasting this thing, this thing called time that we will never get back.

The Sundays on the sofa, watching something you don't like, tweeting, updating your status, posting updates etc., etc. And moaning about another wasted weekend, doing nothing and another boring week ahead.

Monday morning hits and you go back into your Monday to Friday dying syndrome. Social media is filled with quotes, pictures and photos saying 'Don't worry, it's nearly Friday' and from the moment you are out of bed on Monday morning it begins – the weekly death. And it goes a bit like this:

Monday – It's Monday. You hate Monday. You wish it was still the weekend. You don't want to get out of bed, don't want to go to work, can't wait until Friday. No training happens on Mondays, no meetings first thing, but after 10.00 is fine.

Tuesday – You have realised it isn't Monday any more and you should really get on with it. Marketing campaigns work best on Tuesdays as you are more receptive, two or three day courses start, but the Chinese takeaway is closed today and you need to buy dinner.

Wednesday – OMG, it's the middle of the week. It's the middle of the week and you still have two days left until the weekend. It's the middle of the week and you have loads to do before the weekend. You need to get on with it.

Thursday – You still have one day left until Friday. Get through today and it will be Friday tomorrow. You have a few meetings today and you realise you now only have one day left to complete everything you need to do, especially because the rest of the week has been spent counting down how many days you have left this week until the weekend.

Friday – Woohoo, only eight, maybe seven, maybe six hours left until the weekend depending on how quickly you can get things done and then you head off early. Luckily the last meeting of the day has cancelled so if you finish everything by three, you can sneak out and then it's Saturday, woohoo!!

Sounds familiar? Do you recognise this in yourself, your team, maybe your boss?

Maybe if you do think like this, you are not doing something you love. Maybe you are putting things off. Maybe you are wasting precious time.

I have worked with and for companies where the week outlined above is part of the weekly mantra for the staff and the managers. And a lot of these companies, then recruit consultants to come in and tell them what's wrong and provide a 'here's one I prepared earlier' solution.

I have written this book with you the individual in mind. The tips and techniques in this book allow you, the individual reading it, to take some or all of the tips I have used in my business, my home and my life, and make them work for you and your life. They allow you to take control of your own time and make every minute count – or as near as you can possibly get.

This doesn't mean you can't be spontaneous and leave work early, or head to the cinema or for a walk or a long lunch – in fact, it's quite the opposite. Because you will be making more time in your life for the important stuff and you are more focused and more determined to get things done, you will have more time to do things on the spur of the moment and enjoy life more, every precious second.

I read that Barack Obama spends two hours a day thinking and reflecting; time to himself, time to be creative by himself. I'm not at the two hour stage quite yet, but I do make time and space for thinking.

When I was employed, I used the commute home as this space and it worked. Sometimes the thoughts I had were a bit crazy, but often that was the only space I had had all day and as soon as I was on the train the thoughts flowed.

I used to wonder why my best thoughts came when I was in the bathroom and then it dawned on me that as, a working mum of twins, it was often the only quiet time I had all day.

Now my sons are older, I manage my time and my workload and I plan some time each day and each week for thinking. I cannot continue to be successful if I do not continue to have thinking time each day And I'm not talking time sat procrastinating or watching rubbish TV. I genuinely mean thinking time. By now you may be thinking it's the impossible dream, but by using the techniques in this book I have found time to allow myself thinking time and quality, regular family time.

Nothing will stop you from being creative so effectively as the fear of making a mistake. — John Cleese

Find your why

You might not call your why, your why. It might be your vision, your purpose, your goal. For me it is my why, and knowing what it is, and why it is, makes everything else so much easier. Planning my time, my priorities, knowing when I am on track and when I'm not – it's all about my why.

And your why can change. Some may disagree with this, but your why can absolutely change depending on where you are in your life, what your focus is and what you want to achieve.

For instance, when I was 18, my why was 'earn more money'. Pretty shallow, but that's what it was. I wanted to buy a car, a house, have holidays, treat my mum and dad, and all of that was dependent on earning more money.

As I became a parent my why became 'looking after my sons'. Again quite simple, but it was as simple as that. That included earning more money, having some me time to keep me sane, doing well at work etc. At this point I will add that I suffered the most horrific post-natal depression that was not diagnosed or treated for several years, and whilst as a functioning depressive I seemed fine and capable on the outside, inside I was a wreck. Drinking too much, pushing away those closest to me, hiding as many things under the rug as I possibly could, but still loving, caring and providing for my sons.

Looking after my sons will always be on my list of things to do but as they get older, it's actually more about just being there. I'm coming to terms with the fact that they no longer want to spend any time with me and would rather be with their friends, and I cherish the time I do have with them. I have learnt over the years that bombarding them with questions doesn't work – they just grunt and shrug their shoulders – but giving them time, space and listening, just as in a coaching relationship, they do the talking. They start the conversation and we can talk for ages. This works best when we walk the dog, which we don't do as a family as often as we should, but there is a point in the road where the conversation always starts so I wait for that point and smile as soon as I hear the word. 'Mum?'

Recently I took my sons to meet up with their friends at different locations. I'd dropped off one son and was taking the other to where he wanted to go, just 10 minutes away. During those 10 minutes he talked about his recent exam results, how school was going and then for the first time told me about his girlfriend. Those 10 minutes of me being silent were precious.

Your why may not come instantly. Sometimes it takes time; sometimes you know instantly. Sometimes you listen to the whys of others and theirs sound so big, so life changing, so 'change the world', that you think yours sounds inferior and that there must be something bigger.

When I started Chrysalis Consulting, the biggest driver aside from wanting to do what I loved doing – the coaching, development and culture change – was that I wanted to be the ethical consultancy. The consultancy that wouldn't just take your money and pull something out a drawer to make it fit, nor the consultancy that would say yes to an assignment just because it would pay the bills. However, I found that hard to market as it just sounded as though I hated everyone else or wanted to say I was better than everyone else. I had also found it hard saying no to some assignments as I really did need my bills paying.

So I thought long and hard and spent months trying to work out what my why was. It was about support, it was about development, change, transformation, challenge but again, nothing particularly tangible.

Then one day I got it! I was at the Aspire MAD Leadership Conference in London with Sam Collins and a room full of MAD women, including the wonderful Diversity Tribe, and I was there as a participant for the two day event and a panel member in the evening. On the second day of the conference, there it was as clear as day: my why was 'creating butterflies'. What? Creating butterflies – providing the space and environment for individuals, teams and businesses to grow as well as the skills and mindset to find their wings and fly on their own.

Butterflies take time to grow and they do so in a safe environment until they are formed and ready to go out into the world with their beautiful wings. And it fits in with home, work and family.

I felt 10 stone lighter as soon as this came to my mind and the more people I shared it with during that day, the more I smiled and the lighter I became.

I tested this with friends and family and they all looked at me like I was mad, but that was it, my why. I started to think about it more though. How could I sell that? What about the corporates, the big guns that I wanted to work with? How would they buy that?

My husband, my sons and a few male colleagues also informed me that it sounded too feminine and so for them, they would steer clear. At that point part of me thought 'So what?' The people I had asked clearly weren't my customers – but they were. They were exactly the sort of clients I wanted to work with. More and more people, particularly women, are leaving the corporate world and starting their own businesses or just not working and many of those left are experiencing the Monday to Friday dying that I highlighted in the previous chapter. If the corporates keep losing talent and retaining those that are dying a slow and painful Monday to Friday death, what happens to the corporates, our economy and the labour market? These were exactly the clients that I wanted to work with, but how could I sell them butterflies?

It was during my meeting with Becky that I gained more clarity, and I gained even more at a meeting with Gail Thomas, my business mentor. I wasn't selling butterflies. The butterflies were an outcome of what I achieved. I did and still do transform individuals and teams and businesses, and I equip them with the skills and mindset to fly on their own, rather than creating a dependency, or causing too much reliance. I don't ever want to be the person that has been coaching someone for 16 years with very little change or development in my client, or having a situation where my client cannot or will not make a decision without having to run it by me first. That is not a healthy relationship. That is not coaching and that is not development.

So what then is my why? Quite simply, you have already read it. What is the one thing that makes me mad, frustrated, even angry when is it wasted? Time. I give people the gift of time by allowing them to use it more effectively but, coupled with this, I create environments and encourage more effective communication.

That is it – my why. We are the ethical consultancy that will not work with you if we genuinely do not believe we can help. But through everything we do, the HR, the coaching, the culture change and the development workshops, it is all about giving you time back. Making you, your team or your business more effective, more efficient, more accountable, more aligned – whatever it is, it is about giving you back time and finding ways to communicate effectively.

One of my clients was struggling with her why. She couldn't think of anything ground breaking, anything that would set the world on fire, and so she started to doubt herself and felt herself worthless and not capable of carrying on with the senior position she was working in. As she talked and I listened, I could hear she did have a why and it was a very powerful why; her why is about providing opportunities for others. She does this at home, through her role, through her challenging many of the working practices in her company, by championing and paving the way for others to follow in her footsteps, for developing herself, for working with her mentees; it is all about providing opportunities for others.

She had spent months questioning herself and looking for something groundbreaking, yet in one hour she found her why and moved forwards with purpose, and in her life and her company this was groundbreaking.

Another of my clients seemed to be in the shoes of 18-year-old me when they were trying to figure out their why: it all came back to money. But as we dug a little deeper, it was about money that would grow a business that was supporting and providing opportunities for young people in the City. That's a pretty big why and again it was resolved in an hour, just by making the time, having a focus and not wasting time worrying about what it should look like and whether it was groundbreaking enough.

For others, it's as simple as making marketing more simple or creating better environments.

Your why will be in your gut rather than in your head. Your head will come out with all sorts of information and produce mission statements so long that you need a six foot banner to write them on. The head always tries to make the why into something understandable, something you can market, something you can sell or explain.

Go with your gut. What really makes you tick? What is it that you are passionate about? That can be a happy kind of passionate, like I am with developing people, or the mad passion with which I hate time wasters and those than can but don't communicate. What is it that really turns your gut with excitement?

That's your why.

Your why is your sense of purpose, for what you are doing in your job or creating in your life. It is your passion. And it shouldn't be about just your career but in every area of your life. After all, you are a whole person.

So if you were to ask me 'Who are you?' I would respond by saying 'I am the giver of time and effective communication.' You may want to know more about me and how I could do that, or you may think I am completely bonkers.

Stop! ACTION POINTS

Take some time and ask yourself 'Who am I?' Keep going until you have run out of answers.

Ask yourself 'What's my why?'

Identify why you do what you do and write down some actions.

Identify what difference you are making for yourself and for others.

.

I always wonder why birds stay in the same place when they can fly anywhere on the earth. Then I ask myself the same question. — Hurun Yahya

Know your strategy

For what? You might be asking 'What do I need a strategy for?' Well, you now know your why, which is fantastic – congratulations on defining your purpose, vision, mission, whatever you have chosen to call it – but what next?

How do you know that what you are doing, thinking and saying is right and aligned to your why and how do you start to make your why happen?

Because you will have a strategy.

In the next chapter where we look at mindset I will provide you with some further information, some questions that I use to support my strategy and allow me to know I am on the right step, but for now let's stick with this.

I have a clear focus on what I do every day and how I show up every day. This will always be a bit of a work in progress but I have built my resilience and my ability to handle most situations with ease and deep confidence AND I have created habits that support and renew me on a daily basis. How? By having a strategy.

If, like me, you have a why based on time with one of the outcomes being about transformation and change, you really can't be a time waster; you can't be afraid of change or challenging the status quo. If, like some of my clients, your why is about creating opportunities for others or making marketing simple, you can't sit back and do nothing or overcomplicate things for yourself and others.

You need to have alignment.

When I say I am a work in progress around the strategy, I really do mean it. I hate to waste time, I hate being late, I like to be busy, I like to develop myself and learn and my brain is always coming up with new ideas, new ways of doing things, new workshops to deliver. And in amongst all of this, I am a bit of a control freak.

This doesn't mean I don't delegate; I do, and I delegate well. It doesn't mean that I have to do everything, although sometimes it does, and on occasions it means I don't ask for help at the right time. I go into machine mode thinking that in order to get things done it has to be done by me. As a result, some of the things that I am not particularly strong at, or that I enjoy, or that get me closer to my why, I do. It happens less and less but it does still happen. I am a work in progress.

When I do that I then think, 'What on earth am I doing?' because actually all I am doing is wasting my time. Which, if you have been paying attention so far, is something I do not like, do not agree with and actually get very frustrated about, so whilst I am getting better, I need to watch this.

And so do many of my clients. For those of us where time is part of our why, we often fall into the trap of thinking that by doing it ourselves it will be quicker – and in a lot of cases that may be true – but actually, I am a visionary leader. I do big picture, I do solutions, I do support, I delegate. I do not do detail particularly well, I am not a natural administrator, I am not a completer finisher. And whilst there have been times when I have thought that it is quicker for me to do something than explain to someone else what needs doing, someone that has detail or administration as a natural talent may complete it in 30 minutes whereas it might take me a day. Where is the sense in that?

So your strategy: provide the stepping stones on the path to your why. If I continue to do things that I know I am not good at, I am wasting time and money.

If my clients continue to do things the way they have always done them, instead of looking at newer, faster, better ways, then they are wasting time and money. And the gift of time that I give back to them could be better spent on the big picture, on pleasing more customers or on engaging with more staff. It is their gift to do with what they wish.

As part of my strategy there is no longer a work me and a home me. I no longer have to wear a mask at home or at work. I am me, the total person, me. For some of you this will make sense.

You leave for work, and often because of your position within the company or your boss or your team, you put on the work mask. The one that says I have not been up all night with the kids or had a fight with my partner, the one that will never discuss what happened over the weekend or where you are going on holiday. The mask that hides any emotion or thoughts or, in some cases, personality. The mask that says I am at work, the mask that goes very well with the suit that says I am at work and the shoes and possibly the handbag or manbag, depending on which you prefer.

Then on your way home you try and remove this mask but it can be stuck on a little too tightly. Behind it are the pressures and the conversations you have spent all day having. Perhaps you have had to let someone go or discipline someone; perhaps there was a difficult conversation with a customer or your boss. Maybe you had a great day but because you are having some difficulties at home, you don't want to walk in with a big smile plastered all over your face or vice versa.

So on your journey home, you try to prize off the mask – it's coming loose, that's it, just a little more – and sometimes when you arrive home it's off, sometimes it's loose and sometimes it's still so rigidly stuck to your face that over dinner you get remarks like 'I am not one of your team' as you ask your partner to pass you the potatoes, and you know this is going to be a long, long night.

For those of us that have or do wear masks, whether you know it or not, you have a strategy for dealing with the masks and what is behind them. You have a strategy for what to say to whom and when and which information you hold back and which you share, for what you wear to which event and when. You have a strategy.

I remember when I would be the one at work that always dressed a bit more quirkily, a bit more differently to everyone else. Everyone would comment on my outfits and how they liked them and that they reflected my personality and then one day, I was invited to an event with my Chief Exec and I was told that I needed to wear a black dress. I didn't even own a black dress, I told him, and I laughed it off but he looked at me and suggested very strongly that I wear a black dress. That was it! I had been sucked into the corporate suit division where only black, grey and navy were permitted in the workplace. Where any personality had been immediately sucked from me at the door as I entered. I'm exaggerating of course, but there is nothing more depressing than walking into a meeting room where the only colour you see are the sneaky red socks that the guy sitting opposite you has worn to create a stir.

CREATE YOUR PURPOSE, MANAGE YOUR TIME

The current bliss for me is that I no longer wear a mask; I don't feel I have to and I have nobody telling me that I need to, and this saves me time. Being authentic all of the time saves me time and I like that.

I recently spent some time working with an image consultant who matched my colours and my style of clothes to who I am. A couple of days later I was delighted when I went to the biggest meeting of my business career to date in a lime green top and was offered the contract. It was so refreshing.

And I don't need to pretend to be fine when I'm not, or pretend to be solemn when I am not: I am me. I can be me with my clients, my team, my family and my friends. It feels wonderful and saves time.

If you are reading this and thinking 'I was always able to do that,' then I envy you. However, I was one of the unlucky ones who worked at companies where any life that didn't represent the corporate DNA of the company was sucked out of you. Like a stick of rock, I had the name of the company running through me – but my name and my individuality had gone.

So part of my strategy is to be me, all the time, and ensure I ask for help when needed, as well as thinking in advance about whether I am the best person for the task in hand or not. If it doesn't play to my strengths, and it doesn't get me one step closer to my why, then I don't do it. Sounds easy? It isn't, but with practice and a clear line of accountability, which we will come onto later, you can do it.

You may not be in the same position as me, with your own company, so as I said at the beginning of the book, it is for you to take the tips I provide, make them your own and make them work for you, which I hope you will be able to do.

My strategy also involves my message being clear and identifying my ideal client. Some of you may not have the luxury of selecting your clients or customers, but whether you do or you don't, I hope you provide an excellent service to whoever your clients are.

Part of my strategy, particularly for my business, is knowing who my ideal customers are. I have worked with Sam, Becky and Gail on this and again this was not an easy process but in the long run it has saved me time, money and energy. Because I want to help people to grow and not waste anyone's time, I initially wanted to work with anyone. After all, we can all develop further and improve the way we communicate and a strong effective culture should be at the heart of every business.

The trouble is, anyone could mean literally anyone so how do you find them and how do they find you? You have to narrow it down. When I first started my company, I remember all the guys that had been in business for 30 years or more telling me I needed a niche. To some extent they were right, but they wanted me to narrow it down to the smallest minutiae of detail and say something like, 'It's women between the ages of 20 and 35.' This I couldn't do. Firstly I didn't want to limit what I do to individuals, then I didn't want to limit it to gender or age and so my demographic kept getting bigger.

My ideal client is someone who is passionate about change. Someone who wants to gain back more time to do with it as they wish. Someone who is committed to delivering a better service to customers and staff. Someone who wants to increase business performance.

I then hear from a lot of potential clients, 'Well, that's me you are talking about,' but when you dig a little deeper, they don't want to change. They don't want to question or challenge how things are done or identify more efficient ways of doing things, so I let them know they aren't ready and either they commit that they are or we agree to part company. You may think that this contradicts what I said earlier about tailor-made solutions, but it doesn't. I identify with my clients what is needed, and why, and sometimes this is not always what is wanted, but if I think this will waste them time and money, I walk away. Time is precious.

I can gauge very quickly how receptive people are to change and whether they really want the change they say they do, and within a day, I know whether I have found my ideal client. If I cannot help I say so and I leave. Time is precious, and I won't waste it.

I did once; I wasted a few years. I started at one company and on my first day I knew I had made a mistake. I wasn't expected, the IT access took more than two weeks to sort, and I knew this wasn't for me, but deep down, like the cinema theory, I tried to convince myself things would get better. They did for a short while but only in the areas I had improved; everything else remained the same or got worse. From then on, I have stuck with my gut and I know within a day whether it is a yes or no. This is part of my strategy and it works for my clients and me.

One thing, however, that I thought I was ready for, and I almost was but not quite, was the impact of this one day rule, the search for my ideal customer and the Marmite effect.

At school, I was 'Marmite'. The adverts 'My mate Marmite' struck a chord with me and my friends and I suppose the closer you analysed it, the more I became like Marmite. You either loved me or you hated me; there wasn't really a kind of like or kind of don't like, it was one scale or the other. I started to build up a resilience around this but in reality as a teenager you want everyone to like you. The outer core was saying I'm this and I'm proud, whilst the inner was screaming out, just wanting to be liked.

As I started my career though, the Marmite effect became even more apparent. And the more senior I became in my roles, the more resilient I became and the need to be liked lessened and so the Marmite effect continued and to this day sticks with me.

It's difficult though, when you are in the early stages of starting a company. You want people to like you and what you do and what you offer and how you do things. You don't understand why people would look at your wonderful website and not want to buy from you instantly (do they not know how much effort went into it!!). You want people at the networking events you go to to say WOW, you are wonderful and of course I want to work with you – and then you wake up. The deeper you look, and the more that you know and understand about yourself, you realise you don't want to work with just anyone, you won't appeal to everyone and so the Marmite effect continues. And it feels at times as though it burns a little deeper, particularly as this is your business, your money, your bills that need paying at the and of the month and you want to reach your why.

This is where the strategy comes in very handy. When you start to doubt your path, or question your actions, or question the results, always go back to your strategy. It may or may not be a long lengthy document. It might be a few words or statements that you understand enough to keep you on track; it could be a vision board, a scribbled notepad, a spreadsheet.

I have a document, just one page, a vision board, and my website as a reminder. I also use quotes – useful, relevant quotes – as reminders, and I have them stuck all over my desk. I know my why and I know my what. I am clear that I no longer care what others think of me. I just ask myself each day, 'Is this getting me closer to my why?' If it is, I keep going; if it isn't, I stop it.

Stop! ACTION POINTS

Take some time and ask yourself what you need to do to get closer to your why.

Write down some points on what your strategy is.

Consider and move forwards with one action that you can take today, right now, that will help you in some way.

It is only when we truly know and understand that we have a limited time on earth — and that we have no way of knowing when our time is up — that we begin to live each day to the fullest, as if it was the only time we had —
Elizabeth Kubler-Ross

The right mindset

Mindset can be a funny thing. We often know, or think we know, what we should be doing and why we should be doing it. Often, however, despite knowing what and when we should do things, we have voices in our head. These voices can cause doubt, stop us taking action, tell us to wait until tomorrow or not to worry about doing things now, the time isn't quite right, we should wait for everything to be perfect before we take action. This can then lead to feelings of overwhelm as things start to mount up around us or as the to-do list grows and grows or we wake up and realise that it may be too late to do the things we wanted.

I carried around a strong fear of failure for years. I told myself this fear was my protection. It was there to ensure that I didn't fail, that I didn't do things I couldn't do or things that would make me look or feel foolish.

I have always been lucky to have a number of strong role models in my life – my parents, teachers, managers, business people I respected – and fear of failure, as I was often told, was something to hold on to. After all, a fear of failure would and could only ensure that I didn't fail. And by not wanting to fail, or having this fear holding me back from failing, it would be almost impossible for me to fail in anything I said or did. And I believed it. Who wouldn't? After all, this fear, as with any fear, was there to protect me and keep me safe, right?

Wrong!

It took me years to learn this was wrong. Yet until I realised it was wrong, everyone I had ever spoken to about it, the interview panels I had spoken to about it, the development reviews I had raised it in, all told me fear of failure was a good thing to have as it would ensure my success.

Not long after I started to learn more about coaching and the benefit of powerful questions did I start to question my own fear. This fear of failure that had been protecting me for so long, looking after me, keeping me safe and on the road to success – how had it really helped me?

The truth was it hadn't at all. My fear of failure meant there had been many occasions where I hadn't taken myself out of my comfort zone in case I failed. There were times I hadn't taken risks in case I failed. There were times I hadn't spoken up, times I had gone against my gut and walked away from difficulties, all because of a fear of failure.

How could I truly learn if I never failed? How could I be truly successful if I never failed? The truth was I couldn't.

As I questioned my fear, I started to ask myself how I could turn this into a positive and really use it to my advantage. I wrote down lists and then it came. The light bulb switched on inside my head. What if my fear of failure was no longer a fear of failure but a determination to succeed?

My intuition told me this was right, my brain started whirring and I knew instantly I was on the right path.

If I had a determination to succeed rather than a fear of failing, I could make mistakes as long as learning from them got me one step closer to succeeding. I could take risks if they got me one step closer to succeeding. I could speak up, walk into difficulties, do things that scared me – terrified me, even – and continue to grow as a person, a mum, a wife, a daughter, a leader, a coach and a facilitator, because I had a determination to succeed, and this was something that would not only benefit me, but also my family, friends and colleagues.

Every experience, good or bad, is a stepping stone on the road to success.

Fear of failure comes up for many of my clients during one-to-one coaching, through development workshops and often through culture change. The 'what if' scenario. What if we are moving the business in the wrong direction, what if people aren't on board with it, what if it goes wrong?

The feelings of unrest, anxiety, confusion and sometimes anger this can create are overwhelming. But what is the worst that can happen? It goes wrong. OK – acknowledge it, review what went wrong and do it better next time. Everything becomes a stepping stone on the path to success.

I'm not for one minute saying that everyone has this fear, but I am sure that some of us have a fear of some sort. How can you reframe yours into a positive to stop it from holding you back?

I have overcome the fears, doubts, limiting beliefs or insecurities that were holding me back. And I have created a new set of empowering beliefs to support me as I create the next stage of my life. Not an easy task, and certainly more and more will come from this: remember, it's all a work in progress.

It's not just fear that can hold us back. In the opening paragraph, I highlighted that sometimes we are waiting: waiting for everything to be perfect, the right conditions, the right time. Yes, they may be important, but how do you know if they are right?

What's your gut telling you? If your gut is telling you to go for it but the voices in your head say wait, which do you listen to?

Over the decades, we humans have turned off our intuition, or chosen to ignore it when we feel it. Some of us have lost the ability to be intuitive altogether and this can often be what causes the self-doubt to creep in. Our gut tells us one thing and our head tells us something different.

As we regularly believe that our head is making a decision based on evidence, facts, a similar situation, we usually go with that. At least that way, if we have to justify a decision or action, we can use the evidence to back it up, which will surely help.

Taking into consideration my HR background, there were often times when I ignored my gut or looked for ways to justify my decisions.

For example, in interviews I would know if someone was right for the job, I just knew. Something about them said yes or no. But I needed the evidence to back this up and if I couldn't find it, my gut feeling sometimes had to be ignored. Why?

Imagine me receiving a claim for an unfair selection process. The candidate with the highest scores in the process didn't get the job because my gut told me they weren't right and I would have to justify this to a judge at an employment tribunal. Not an easy process to have to go through, nor one I would ever want to put myself in.

Don't get me wrong: I would raise my 'gut feeling'. I would mention that there was something I couldn't always put my finger on, that I just had a feeling. And before long the successful applicant whom I had my gut feeling about would do or say something that proved me right not long after they were appointed.

If there was evidence to back up my feeling but others in the room were not so sure, we may look at other candidates or have a follow up interview or an informal chat – but to this day, my 'gut' has never been wrong in an interview.

Recently, I was on the way to pick up my sister from a train station about 50 miles away from where I live and I ignored my gut. I was in the car, radio playing, sat nav telling me which way I was going, and as I approached a junction on the motorway, my intuition was telling me I needed to turn off. I had no idea why, so I checked the sat nav and as it was telling me to stay on the road and take the next junction I carried on. The closer I got to the first junction, however, the stronger my gut was telling me to turn off early, but I carried on. I carried on convinced that the electronic device knew better and clearly it was a much better route. After all, the next junction, the one that I was being instructed to take by my friendly electronic device, was only four miles away. I convinced myself it knew best and I carried on.

And then it happened.

There had not been a single sign – no warning, no flashes on the motorway signs – but the junction I was being told to take was closed. Just like that: a sign a mile before my junction saying 'slip road closed'. The following junction was 10 miles further on and I had no choice but to carry on along the motorway, 10 miles further than I needed to go, still following my sat nav that was rerouting all the way. I watched my estimated arrival time increase by 34 minutes. My sister would be waiting for half an hour on the platform and I had promised her I would be there.

I continued, turned off at the next junction, pulled over and called her. Luckily her train had been slightly delayed so she wouldn't have to wait long for me but if I had followed my intuition I would have been there waiting as I said I would.

In the end she didn't have to wait as I arrived a couple of minutes before her, but for someone who values time, hates to waste it, hates to keep people waiting and hates to be late, I knew if I had followed my gut I would have been there earlier.

Other than the recent sat nav trusting experience, which I will aim to never let happen again, I have four questions that I *usually* ask myself before making a decision or taking action and they help me greatly in moving in the right direction.

1. How will this get me closer to my purpose?

2. How will this help me in helping others?

3. Is it a priority?

4. Can I delegate it?

It will be important for you to find your own questions; maybe you don't need as many as four, or maybe you need a few more. Whatever the questions, they need to work for you.

Let me share why these work for me.

I'm a big picture thinker and often I have 100 ideas going round in my head for a new workshop or a new way to decorate the living room or help a charity etc. Sometimes I need to ignore the random thoughts and concentrate on what I am doing; sometimes I don't. On other occasions, I may just feel like sitting and reading all day or watching rubbish TV or staying in bed. Whatever thoughts I have, I ask the questions.

Say, for example, today I feel like staying in bed because I am drained. It's been a long week and this morning I can't be bothered to move. The answers will of course vary depending on the day and the situation, but it could go like this:

1. How will this get me closer to my purpose? – Because I need to rest in order for me to be fully present and focused with my clients and it has been a really busy week.

2. How will this help me in helping others? – Because I often speak about the need to look after yourself and rest in order to be able to focus. By following what I see as important for others, it re-emphasises the importance and I can use today as an example next time someone asks about it or says it is impossible.

3. Is it a priority? - Yes, I am delivering a presentation this evening and some rest will do me good. There is nothing in the diary that can't wait.

4. Can I delegate it? – No, but I can delegate some of the admin tasks I was going to do later. They always take me forever anyway as I am not particularly detail-focused and I do not understand the formatting.

Or it could look like this:

1. How will this get me closer to my purpose? – Because I need to rest in order for me to be fully present and focused with my clients and it has been a really busy week.

2. How will this help me in helping others? – Because I often speak about the need to look after yourself and rest when needed in order to be able to focus. By following what I see as important for others, it re-emphasises the importance and I can use today as an example next time someone asks about it or says it is impossible.

3. Is it a priority? - No. I have to finish designing the workshop for next week and I can't postpone anything in my diary this week.

4. Can I delegate it? – No.

Scenario 1 has an answer called 'stay in bed'. I only ever do for an hour or so anyway and as I struggle to sleep, I may doze off for a second but then usually lie in bed listening to the radio or reading. This is my idea of resting, so is most welcome. And don't get me wrong, the 'do later' will be done later; it won't be put off until tomorrow.

Scenario 2 produced an answer called 'get up now', which I do, and quickly so I'm not late.

As I said, the situations can vary but these questions help me in getting out of bed as much as they do making a very important, strategic, possibly life changing decision.

Your questions must be yours so you know they will work for you. I have a client that asks one question: 'Is this a priority?' Just this one question helps him to make a decision – the right decision for him – and then he moves on.

This won't work for everyone, as you could find yourself answering yes to this each time. The client in question is very good at prioritising and knows his long-term vision and purpose inside out and back to front and he has spent years getting to this point, so for him this works.

I know for me it absolutely wouldn't, but if I ask the first two questions I am then able to quantify priority or not.

Stop! ACTION POINTS

Write down your questions that will help you when making decisions.

Think about what it will take for you to follow your gut.

Consider the voices of self-doubt that are living nicely in your head and think about what you will do to tell them to stop talking or at least quieten down a little.

Write down any fears that are currently holding you back that you need to turn around to get you moving in the right direction.

We all have exactly the same amount of time every single day, so you have to put yourself in the right frame of mind to utilise that time to the very best of your ability. That starts by you realising that you are in control.

What's in your toolbox?

What on earth does this mean, you might be asking?

Let's give a few examples:

Imagine you are a plumber. You have a toolbox and it's filled with tools: a screwdriver or two, a wrench, maybe a plunger, a first aid kit. To have someone book you for a job you also need a phone, an address for the job and some form of transport to get you there. What else?

You'll have some (hopefully excellent) customer service ability. You know your prices, whether fixed or hourly. You might have a sat nav. You will also have experience, knowledge and skills, and maybe other connections or contacts to call on if you need to, on the odd occasion that you find yourself in a bit of difficulty or need some advice. You will have your qualifications, and then you have yourself. You know what you are and are not capable of. Perhaps whilst you are there you are asked to do some electrical work. Hopefully you will know your own limitations and whether or not you can say yes to this, and then you can get on with the job.

Now imagine that you are a parent and you are taking the kids to the zoo for the day. Sounds simple – you get in the car and go. Yeah right, I hear you say! This will of course depend on how old the children are, but it could be you are still waiting for the day when you can just get in the car and go rather than go through the military exercise that is required. So you are taking the kids to the zoo. What's in your toolbox?

You and the kids, for starters. Then maybe nappies, bottles, bibs, a change of clothes, packed lunch, snacks, nibbles, maybe some in-car entertainment, a vehicle, a map or a sat nav, your wallet.

You may have bought tickets in advance; you might have researched the route and how long it will take, and correlated this to the zoo's opening time, so you know when to leave. You may have already looked up the types of animals so you can talk to the kids about them all; you may have planned which way you will go round. You might have spoken to friends or family about the trip and heard some anecdotes or stories about the time they visited and what they enjoyed or disliked about it. Maybe they have told you all the negatives of their experience – that it rained all day, some of the enclosures were closed; you know the people who always give you the negative side to every story (we will come back to these type of people in a later chapter). Maybe you went as a child and loved it. And off you go, on your fabulous day out, with a toolbox full of stuff and information.

Now let's imagine you hold a senior role in a successful company that has just gone through a round of redundancies as some of the middle managers were no longer required and the structure needed to be minimised for cost and time efficiencies. Some of the managers that left were in your team; you followed the process and did everything you needed to. Only you know whether you agreed with the process but it's done and now you have a really large project to deliver in a tight timeframe.

What's in your toolbox?

The project outline and objectives, your team, your deadline date, budget, resources, everything else you need to get done, maybe – and then you panic.

Why?

Because for some of us, we only look at what is in the toolbox directly in front of us when we really need to see the bigger picture.

Our plumber doesn't panic or say he doesn't have the time; he just gets on with it. It's his job.

On the way to the zoo, our parents may panic when they need the third change of clothes for the kids that they talked themselves out of bringing as they didn't want to be weighed down quite so much all day, but on the whole they get on with it. They planned, they packed, they researched they went, and they had a great day – in spite of the energy vampires telling them it would be awful (more about this in a later chapter).

Both the parents and the plumber knew what they had available to them, used it and delivered.

All too often, I have seen changes made in companies to processes, budgets or structures and as soon as the next big piece of work comes, so does the panic. We start thinking, 'I can't do that, they have just taken most of my team away,' and time is wasted arguing or disagreeing constructively with senior colleagues, explaining why it can't be done, that nobody has the time or the skills or the knowledge or the capacity to take on a project at this time – and we procrastinate. And then we go home or out after work and waste time and energy telling anyone that will listen that we don't have the time or the energy for this project. However, we never seem to question why we are wasting our time or energy talking about the fact that we don't have the time or energy!

Let's look at what's in your toolbox.

You have a project, a timeframe, a budget, your team, maybe other people in the organisation who would love to get involved. You have your skills, your experience, your knowledge, your background, other people around you, maybe a mentor or a coach or your boss, your intuition.

All of these things will help you. Sometimes we just need to delve a little deeper, see the bigger picture and stop wasting time panicking.

A client of mine was in this state of panic after exactly this situation and he spoke for a while about his weaknesses that some of his departing colleagues had as strengths, and that now they weren't there, he couldn't deliver the project.

We explored how this project could develop his weaknesses (I prefer the term 'development areas'; my only real weakness is chocolate!) and how he could identify colleagues and peers from across the business who may also have development areas that they want to work on, but who could bring some additional strengths too.

We discussed how his manager may perceive him if, the first time he is asked to deliver a piece of work after the changes, he were to go straight in with the 'I can't do this' conversation.

We explored his toolbox and every time he spoke, he listed something else he could add. By the end of our conversation, the project seemed so simple: hard work, yes but less complicated and with a lot less panic. There was a plan, a way forward, a toolbox full of skills, experience, development areas, strengths, people, gut feel, budget, resources, a longer than required timeframe and a project that could be achieved ahead of time, to budget and to a really high standard.

In this case, the use of an hour to talk this through saved days if not weeks of panic, procrastination and negativity and created a 'yes I can' attitude and focus.

In between our sessions, my client said he 'woke up' and imagined he was now a plumber. He had this full toolbox and whilst he may not need every single 'tool' for everything he did, he had these tools at his disposal to use, call upon and improve when he needed them. He felt elated!

Until this shift in thinking, he would ordinarily panic, procrastinate, and consider what he needed, how long for, why he needed it etc. He now realised he didn't need all of the answers immediately: given his position in the company, he could explore which tools worked best for which projects or tasks. He realised he needed a bit of thinking time and that to allow this, he needed to delegate more effectively and that through delegating, freeing up time and having his toolbox, he was more effective, more efficient and more of a leader. He needed to get off the hamster wheel for a short time and focus.

I have identified the skills and strengths I need to build and work on regularly to equip me with all of the tools I need to get to the next level. By no means am I perfect (as I have said before) but by recognising what my strengths and development areas are, I know where to focus my time and attention, where to seek help and where I can support and help others. I also know which of my transferable skills I can utilise and adapt to suit different situations.

Stop! ACTION POINTS

Look at the tools and people you have in your life right now and list how they currently can or do help you.

Consider a situation when you could/should have used these and didn't, and write down what would have been different if you had used the tools at your disposal.

Identify any missing tools that you need to gain to aid your success.

Awesome life tip:

Wherever you are right now, it's exactly where you need to be. Whatever you're experiencing right now, it's exactly what you need to be experiencing. You may not be able to see the lesson or the gift in it but it's there, I promise you. You're learning, growing, shifting, changing and becoming more of who you're truly meant to be.

Who are your angels and your vampires?

Have I finally lost the plot, you may be asking? Quite possibly, yes! But what do I mean by angels and vampires?

Last November I was involved in a group coaching programme. I knew where I wanted to go in my career and I knew my strengths, the tools available to me, my vision, my purpose and my lifelong ambition, but one of our group coaching calls followed one of the most draining days of my entire career.

A member of my team was having difficulty in engaging with a member of the executive team. Although he was coming up with lots of good ideas they were being ignored and the Executive had been asking other people to deliver for her. I had waited several weeks to finally get some time in her diary and discuss this, but I was not prepared for the conversation that followed.

The meeting had been going fairly well until I asked her why she was excluding the member of my team and me from all of the work we were trying to assist her with, and why she was asking others to get involved when it was not their role to do so, nor were they skilled enough to do it. The reaction was completely unexpected; she stated that I didn't listen, didn't do as she wanted, that my team were all the same and that she was getting people to do what she wanted in the way she wanted it doing.

The difficulty with this was that what she wanted wasn't in line with what the organisation wanted. It was worlds apart. She continued to talk about the lack of engagement, the lack of accountability within my team, yet every other word she said shocked me more and more. Perhaps my team and I could have done more to try and gain her buy-in to the bigger picture but actually everything she said reflected her and her team, not the other way round.

Now at this point you may be thinking I am shirking my responsibility to acknowledge the faults within my team, but I'm not. I know where we went wrong and I know where we did well. She was blind to her faults and those of her team, which were costing time and money and reflecting badly on the company. We had identified that her management staff were bullying their teams and the staff turnover, grievances and absences in this area of the business was sky high, yet she still tried to say this was due to my team.

I sat there for an hour, listening, allowing her space to talk and offload and waiting for my moment to add some perspective to the situation and find a way to work together more effectively. The last thing I wanted (or that the business needed) was yet another person with whom this individual had broken bridges and started a full scale war, and from a selfish perspective, my success depended on being able to influence key stakeholders.

The meeting finished as we both had other appointments and I went straight into a meeting with the Chief Exec's coach. She asked me what was wrong and I explained. She was not surprised and immediately told me she would inform the Chief Exec. I asked her not to; I said I had a meeting with him the following day and I would explain my views, but not the lashing I had just received. I honestly felt like my soul had been sucked up, wrung out and thrown back at me!

When I returned to the office, I had an invite to go back and see the senior exec that had gone in for the kill just a couple of hours earlier. I accepted, thinking we could finally find a way to work together for the good of the business and agree a way forwards. At least this time I would have the opportunity to put my case across.

WRONG!!

In for the kill she went again, and this continued for another hour. I tried to counter every argument she put across but she refused to listen, blamed everything on me and my team, and kept coming out with ludicrous – and I don't say this lightly – lies about how I was behaving. The untruths kept coming and coming and by the end of the day I felt truly and utterly drained.

And it didn't stop there. On the way back to my desk I kept reliving the conversation – though it's not really conversation if it's only one way, is it? It was a barrage of lies, insults and excuses on her part. On the way home, it was still on my mind; I got home, tried to spend the evening focused on my family, and then finally went to bed to switch off. It didn't work. The words were there and I felt more and more drained.

To make matters worse she had then spoken to another senior colleague and said that she had given me a really hard time but that I had been 'stupid enough' to go back for more. How delightful of her!

The following day when I met with the Chief Exec, he knew about the previous day and said he would speak with her as this behaviour was unacceptable. He never did.

I relayed part of this situation on my group coaching call and was advised: 'She is an energy vampire. Try and limit the time you spend with her.'

You see, there are two types of people we encounter in our lives. OK, there are more than two – everyone is an individual, after all – but most fit into two categories: energy angels and energy vampires.

The vampires literally suck the life out of you. They drain you. Now this could be a boss, a colleague, a family member or a friend; maybe this is or has been you. We have all encountered them at some stage.

You approach them full of life and then it starts... They moan, they bring you down, they complain, they may insult you, they lack responsibility – everything is someone else's fault. Their body language shouts at you as they slump over the table or in the chair. If you mention having a bit of a cold these are the people who are having a much worse one; if you are busy, they are busier; when you want to fix a situation, they want to make it worse. You have some idea of who they are now, right? You have encountered them? When it's friends or family, you may have stopped going for drinks with them or are always busy washing your hair when they invite you round for dinner – but what about at work?

You can only cancel or avoid meetings so many times or ignore emails for so long before you actually have to meet or speak with them. And then they trap you in the room, sucking away your energy and your mood until you feel drained.

What's the key?

Spend time with them, but do it infrequently and for short periods, no more than 30 minutes at a time. Prepare as much as you can in advance, get to the point and get out of there while you are still alive. Trust me, it works. Take control.

For every vampire you know, you need double the amount of angels.

Angels are the people who pick you up and provide you with energy. They are not always going to agree with you, or bow down in awe of you – they do not think you are the best thing since sliced bread – but they give you energy.

They talk passionately and with enthusiasm. They may have similar views to you; they may not. But they want things to succeed. The business, the team activity, whatever it is, they want it as much as you, and maybe even more.

Maybe you have shared values or a shared goal; they motivate you. These are the people who you leave a meeting with feeling fired up and energised and ready to go. These are the people who get things done and if there is a problem, they will work with others to solve it rather than shouting you down, blaming you and avoiding any sort of responsibility.

If they are friends, they may be the life and soul of the party, on the dance floor first, last to leave, concerned about the welfare of others. If they are family, they don't tell you all of their problems during the whole of your visit; they may tell you honestly how they are but will then say something like 'Enough about me, how are you doing?'

If they are your boss or colleague, you love it when you know you are meeting them. You want to spend as much time with them as possible and if you do feel drained by the end of the meeting, it's because there was so much passion and energy in the room, it's because you came up with so many great ideas you now need to calm down, work out exactly what is feasible and deliver it. These are your angels. Know some? Great. Tap into them more and spend as much time with them as possible. If you are self-employed, find angels in networks, or peers with similar experiences, or get a coach or a mentor.

We will all encounter vampires somewhere along the line. In fact, you yourself may have been one at some point, even if just for a short while. Genuinely, the key is to limit your time with them. Being drained does not motivate you to manage yourself or your team effectively. It does not allow for effective communication, as your mind may be elsewhere, worrying about the last vampire encounter or the next one. Vampires hinder your productivity as you sit there feeling sorry for yourself, looking at your to-do list and thinking it's impossible, you will never get it all done, procrastinating more and more and feeling more and more drained as you watch the clock and perhaps look for the stash of sugary snacks to give you a bit of a sugar rush.

Vampires do nothing for your work-life balance. They take over everything and remain in your mind for a long time – and the longer you let them linger, the more harm they will do.

Angels, on the other hand, lift your mood and your spirits. They are the people who put you in a good mood and encourage you to be more productive. The people who inspire you and motivate you to get things done. The people with whom you feel on top of the world. The people you enjoy working with, and want to collaborate with. The people who support others and lead from the front.

These are your angels. Find them and track them down. If you don't have any in your life right now, look for them. Spending time with angels helps you become an angel. You don't want to become a vampire.

I have a number of angels in my life. Elaine and Rachel, who I met during our group coaching and who always pick up my mood on a gloomy day. My fabulous Diversity Tribe, who inspire and motivate me on a daily basis. I met this tribe on a two day workshop and I just know we will be with each other for a very long time to come.

And my sons.

As for everyone else in my life, it really depends on the situation: sometimes they are vampires and sometimes they are angels. However, I realise that can also depend on how I feel on any given day, as the way I feel may affect them. My husband, for example, is usually an angel, but when I am being a vampire, he becomes Dracula; it's not a pretty mix.

When you know who are your angels are, tell them. They will listen to what you need and ask how they can help and you can be an angel for them in return. Remember, they are not always going to agree with you but they will give you perspective and hope. We all need as much of that as we can get, don't we?

Do NOT waste time with vampires. You may have to encounter them but limit your time with them; they make you ineffective and you do not have time to waste being ineffective.

Limit your time with them to 30 minutes, 15 ideally, surround yourself with your angels, and get on with it. Your mood is surprisingly good at managing your ability to waste or utilise the time available.

Stop! ACTION POINTS

Write down who are your angels and vampires.

Consider for a few moments how your mood affects your productivity, your time management and your relationships and note down some positive steps to prevent this from happening in future.

List how your angels and vampires change the way you communicate with others and what actions you can take to stop yourself from becoming a vampire.

Identify who will help you become an angel and what you need to do to make this happen.

A man who dares to waste one hour of time has not discovered the value of life
— Charles Darwin

Who is holding you accountable?

You may have a long list of people who hold you accountable – and if you do, great! – but beware of the 'too many cooks' analogy that may mean you don't know your head from your tail if too many people are after you.

I went to a networking event a few months back where the majority of people in the room were sole traders or small business owners. The speaker at the event told us that as we were self-employed, we had nobody to hold us accountable. The talk started with: 'The plus side of being self-employed is that nobody holds you accountable, and the down side of being self-employed is that nobody holds you accountable.' I disagreed with this instantly, and possibly with good reason, because the talk finished with: 'Here's how to be held accountable: join our paid accountability group so we can help you.' I dislike immensely being sold to at networking events as I believe they are about building relationships and providing support, but I know very few of us hold this view.

I am not employed as a director of a large company anymore but I do have people holding me to account. Firstly, I hold myself to account for my actions, my movements and my to-do list. I don't always get it right, granted, but I learn more and more each week. I have my family to hold me to account. If the work stops coming in and I can't afford food, school uniform, clothes, birthday presents, holidays etc. I will know about it. My coach and business mentor hold me to account and question why I have done it this way or not done it that way, but most importantly they keep me on track with the big picture.

My tribe hold me to account on our calls and our LinkedIn group, where I have listed my five priorities and they ensure I am delivering, but probably –and most importantly – my customers keep me accountable. I no longer have a boss to keep me accountable but I have others, although not too many.

If you are self-employed or a small business owner, joining an accountability group or having a coach or mentor may work for you. Maybe it's family, friends or customers that keep you accountable – but never believe that nobody is holding you to account; they are, even if you don't realise it.

The magic with this is communication.

If you are employed, you have your seniors and your juniors and your clients holding you accountable. You have the Board or your teams or your customers to hold you to account – but what does this really mean in reality? Does it mean you can simply say 'I am held to account'? The key to being held accountable is letting people know what you want them to hold you accountable for.

What do I mean by this?

Well, most of us assume we are accountable for tasks, projects and actions and many of us assume we will be held to account for delivering things – but how do we know? Through the work I have done in, with and for companies, accountability is an area where too many assumptions are made. If I ask the question 'How do you know you are accountable?' many cannot answer; they assume, and when they check whether their assumption was correct, it often wasn't.

So what could make it work? Let's look at a couple of examples:

It may be that you have started a new job. The assumption is that you are accountable for delivering the elements of your job description and your boss is accountable for ensuring you deliver.

But what if you don't receive the training or the tools? Do you just sit there for six months and at the end of your probation say, 'Sorry, not my fault, I didn't get anything you told me I would get?'

How about if, on your first day, you told your boss what to hold you to account for, and they told you? 'I want you to hold me to account for the duties on my job description and I will hold you to account for providing the necessary tools and training.'

Sounds clear and straightforward; it eliminates any time wasting conversations, it's to the point and you can move forwards together. Would you be brave enough to do that?

What if, as Chief Exec, you explain to your staff at the next conference that they should hold you to account for developing the strategy or engaging with them, and that you will hold them to account for delivering it, or customer service levels?

Brave enough for that?

What if, whatever your role, you said to your customers that they should hold you to account for delivering your promises and you will hold them to account for meeting the agreed deadlines?

Brave enough?

How much time and energy could you save if everyone knew who they were accountable to and why and then just delivered?

What difference would this make in your workplace?

What difference would this make to you? Your team? Your customers?

So why don't we do this? Why do we make assumptions that everyone knows what is expected of them?

Every political party has a manifesto, a promise, for what they will deliver if elected and what they stand for. Imagine the difference it would make if they were truly held to account by us, the voting public, when they didn't deliver.

Got that thought?

Stop! ACTION POINTS

Take those feelings, the ones you have right now about the government, the thoughts that are going through your mind, and harness them to ensure you hold yourself to account and empower those around you to do the same. Find some time every day or every week to check in, to hold yourself to account and to ensure you are not wasting time.

Write your manifesto – your promise – and consider your audience and the steps you need to take right now.

Identify who is truly holding you to account and write down what more you need from them in order for you to succeed.

Don't say you don't have enough time. You have exactly the same number of hours per day that were given to Helen Keller, Pasteur, Michelangelo, Mother Teresa, Thomas Jefferson and Albert Einstein – Life's little instruction book

What can you say no to?

Ok, we are almost there. By now you should be on the way to understanding your why, your strategy, the tools and people you have available to you, who gives and drains you of energy and who is holding you to account.

Now what?

More action, I'm afraid.

And this is a biggie ... what can you say no to?

I know, you are very busy and very important and you are needed in every meeting and can't let family or friends down, but seriously, what can you say no to?

Earlier in the book we talked about the rubbish film at the cinema that you wished you hadn't stayed for, so let's start there. Next time you are watching a film waiting for it to get better, say no to watching it until the end. The world will not explode, I promise, and when you have stopped watching it, do something you want to do. Do not waste your time – make it count!

My husband had promised he would take me to the ballet on my 18th birthday to watch Swan Lake. For my 21st birthday, I went with my mum and bought the tickets myself. On my 33rd birthday, he bought tickets for us both to watch the Royal Ballet's performance of Romeo and Juliet at the Royal Opera House. I loved it and cannot wait to go back. I already have lots of tickets purchased for future ballets, though my husband will not be coming with me. He endured it for me: it was my birthday, we had a lovely meal and a few drinks but as far as he is concerned, he will not waste any more of his life ever watching the ballet with me. So if anyone is looking for a ballet partner, I have tickets!

When was the last time you had dinner or drinks with people you didn't really want to have dinner or drinks with, and you felt as though you had wasted your whole evening? Don't do it again or, like the vampires, limit the time with those you really don't want to spend it with. Probably most importantly though, we can't choose our family but if you feel this way about friends, can you really call them friends? Something to think about...

Look at your diary right now. Yes, right now.

What does it look like? Is it full? Empty? Is panic setting in, or are you looking at it and thinking you have the most boring life ever?

Honestly now, what can you say no to in your diary? I know you were told that the Wednesday morning meeting is really important, but you don't know any more than that. You don't know what it's about, you haven't got an agenda, and looking at the attendee list you can't see the role that you play – so cancel it. Say no.

What else in your diary can you say no to?

If you can say no to meetings, say no and get in the habit of saying no. If you don't know why it's needed, it doesn't fit in with your strategy and it doesn't get you a step closer to your goal, say no. Perhaps someone else can go on your behalf who would enjoy it or be able to contribute more. If it's not for you say so, and decline. The same as the lunch appointment with the sales rep. We all love a free lunch but if you don't really have the time to meet with the sales rep whilst they try to flatter you and butter you up until you say yes to working with them, say no.

I have been in the position of being in meeting after meeting all day, sometimes all week. There were times when I was told I was critical to the meeting and would play a key role and so I went, only to find out I didn't need to be there at all. And sometimes people only arrange meetings because your diary is so full it seems to be the only way to get any time with you at all; they block out an hour in your diary and really it could have been a five minute call.

When you are constantly in meetings, when are you meant to get the work completed? When do you find the time or the energy to be creative, innovative and engaging? The truth is you don't unless, like me, you save the commute or shower for your bursts of creativity and enlightenment.

When you are in meeting fatigue and possibly with the vampires, how does this affect your productivity, your mood, your ability to not waste time?

If, like the hamster in the wheel, you are waiting for some space to be able to jump off, just do it. Get off the wheel and out of the meetings that you really don't need to be in.

I mentioned earlier that Barack Obama gives himself two hours a day to himself. Thinking time, creative time, focus time, decision time. Now I am not saying you are the President of the United States, but really, if he can do it, why can't you?

I also mentioned that I am not up to two hours a day but I do have an hour a day of thinking time. It's in my diary and I need it. I need it to create workshops, reflect on my coaching, or draft proposals or solutions for clients. It's time to think about the week ahead and whatever else I need to do , it's in my diary and I use it.

One hour a day to think. This allows me to be more productive, more efficient, more effective, more focused and more present.

How much time can you free up?

It's not just meetings I am talking about here, either.

If you know your why and you know your strategy, why are you doing things that don't fit into them?

Like I said earlier, I am not a natural administrator, so I don't do admin. It wastes my time, isn't part of my strategy and won't get me any closer to my why.

Another way I tried to save time involved getting a cleaner and a gardener, but as I would clean and tidy the house and garden before they arrived, I decided I may as well just get on with it. In a weird way, both are quite satisfying, and whatever I don't have time for is delegated to my husband or sons and they do it.

Back to a work perspective. I know who my ideal clients are and I know my why and my strategy and this has allowed me to say no to a large number of smaller networking groups where my ideal clients don't go and don't have connections with those that do. Also, I said earlier that for me, networking is about building relationships. I have two groups that I will continue to go to because of the people and the relationships, but I have said no to the others.

Maybe it's a group or class that you want to stop going to, maybe it's something that you have done every day or every week for years – is it still something you want to continue to say yes to?

I was having a conversation with someone a few months back who was dreading dinner that night. For years they had met up with the same couple every Wednesday and went for dinner or the cinema or sometimes both. This time though, they really didn't want to go. They liked their friends and still wanted to see them but every week was too much. I asked why they hadn't mentioned it to the other couple. The answer was they didn't want to upset them – despite spending four hours with them every week. If they continued to spend four hours with them every Wednesday, that was a total of 208 hours a year – nine days a year! What could you do with nine full days a year? Take a holiday, decorate the house, write a book, start a course?

An hour a week in a meeting where you're not really needed or you don't want to be may not seem like a lot, but fifty two hours a year – almost two working weeks – could make a big difference.

Spending one day a week on admin that I don't do well, and that would probably take someone else an hour to do to a much higher standard, makes no sense.

Stop! ACTION POINTS

Review your why, identify your priorities and find something – maybe for now just one thing – that you can say no to.

Practise saying no to something with family and friends.

Start saying no! Do it now, the next time you are asked to do something that isn't on your list of priorities. And feel free to let me know how this goes; it can be the hardest thing to master.

The ability to concentrate and to use your time well is everything if you want to succeed in business — or almost anywhere else, for that matter — Lee Iacocca

Summary

Know your why – What is your purpose? What are you trying to or wanting to achieve?

Know your strategy – Whether it's a vision board, a list of priorities or an action plan, create your strategy and stick to it.

Know your mindset – Listen to your heart more than your head. Go with your gut. Find some questions that help you deliver your strategy. Turn any fears into a positive.

What's in your toolbox? – Who and what do you have at your disposal that you can make full use of to help to achieve your why?

Who are your angels and vampires? – Limit your time with those that take away your energy and waste your time and spend time with those that energise and inspire you.

Who is holding you accountable? – You can have the longest list in the world of people to hold you to account. Ultimately, this comes down to you – if you are relying on others to do it, let them know so they actually do.

What can you say no to? – Turn down non-important meetings and tasks that do not fit your why or energise you.

Make the most of every day and every opportunity. Don't waste time – it's too precious.

About the author

Kelly Fryer lives in Cambridgeshire with her husband, twin sons, bulldog and two bearded dragons.

She was born in Bedford in 1980, the eldest of three children and with an older brother from her father's first marriage. The family moved to Peterborough in 1987, where she continues to live. She regularly visits Ibiza, where her younger brother and sister live, and actually relaxes whilst she is there.

Growing up, Kelly's parents had a role reversal where her mum worked and her dad stayed at home, winning a 'Housewife of the Year' competition and working at local playgroups and as a 'dinner lady' at her primary school during lunchtimes.

Kelly had her sons at the age of 20; they were unexpected but a very welcome surprise. She was the youngest HR Director in the UK when appointed to the position in 2012.

Kelly is passionate about saving time and money and creating environments where leaders lead, staff are happy, development is a natural part of the company and communication is clear and effective. Kelly believes all of this can be gained with the right culture.

www.chrysalis-consulting.co.uk

10503526R00060

Printed in Great Britain
by Amazon.co.uk, Ltd.,
Marston Gate.